HOLIDAY

RAIMONDO CORTESE

Currency Press,
Sydney

Principal Sponsor

PKF

Chartered Accountants
& Business Advisers

CURRENCY PLAYS

First published in 2009
by Currency Press Pty Ltd,
PO Box 2287, Strawberry Hills, NSW, 2012, Australia
enquiries@currency.com.au
www.currency.com.au
in association with
Griffin Theatre Company, Sydney

NATIONAL LIBRARY OF AUSTRALIA CIP DATA

Author: Cortese, Raimondo.
Title: Holiday / Raimondo Cortese.
ISBN: 9780868198545 (pbk.)
Series: Current theatre series.
Other Authors / Contributors:
                     Griffin Theatre Company.
Dewey Number: A822.3

Typeset by Dean Nottle for Currency Press.
Printed by Ligare Book Printers, Riverwood, NSW.
Cover design by Jeremy Saunders.
Cover shows Paul Lum. Cover photo: Olivia Martin-Maguire.

Contents

DIRECTOR'S NOTE

Holiday began as some kind of cultural investigation into holidaymaking inspired by the images of Western tourists sunning themselves amidst the carnage of the 2004 Boxing Day tsunami. Over the next two years it gradually evolved into a very intimate exploration of the relationship between two men. In this context *Holiday* came to represent not a holiday in any literal sense, but a relationship created free from the rigors and agendas of day-to-day life.

At the same time we wanted to challenge our own theatre practice. We did not want to create an obvious fictional demonstration to illustrate our concerns. We were interested in a documentary approach to performance. The immediate presence of the performers became an integral part of the relationship played out in the piece, created and recreated moment-by-moment. What we began to discover was a subtle and gentle meditation on the spaces between people, on the lives and histories that we carry around every day, and the strange and elusive state of relaxation. I hope you enjoy *Holiday*.

Adriano Cortese
Melbourne

Holiday was first produced by Ranters Theatre at Arts House, North Melbourne, on 9 August 2007, with the following cast:

PAUL	Paul Lum
ARNO	Patrick Moffatt

Concept and Director, Adriano Cortese
Set design, Anna Tregloan
Lighting design, Niklas Pajanti
Sound design, David Franzke
Dramaturgy, Adriano Cortese, Paul Lum, Patrick Moffatt

CHARACTERS

ARNO
PAUL

*The space is non-representational and contains a wading pool, a beach
ball, a chaise lounge and, up front, a couple of bar stools. The actors
have full awareness of the audience. The baroque songs that intersperse
the dialogue are delivered directly to it.*

SONG: 'My Heart Ne'er Leaps with Gladness'.

ARNO: My mum sent me this parcel the other day.
PAUL: What's that?
ARNO: My mum sent me this parcel the other day.
PAUL: In the mail?
ARNO: Yeah.
PAUL: She spot something... out shopping?
ARNO: You know those plastic thingummies?
PAUL: No.
ARNO: The ones you used to find in the cereal.
PAUL: The funny creatures?
ARNO: She sent me a whole bag of them.
PAUL: Why she send you those?
ARNO: I don't know.

   Silence.

   I was looking at the moon the other night.
PAUL: Yeah?
ARNO: Yeah through a telescope... up close. The full moon.
PAUL: I should buy one.
ARNO: You can make them.
PAUL: Not too hard?
ARNO: No... I don't think so.
PAUL: You really need to live in the country.
ARNO: Yeah... too many lights.
PAUL: It must have some effect us.
ARNO: The moon?
PAUL: We're ninety-nine point whatever per cent water.
ARNO: Oh... sure. That's why we like beaches.
PAUL: Right.
ARNO: Ever meet anyone doesn't like the beach?

PAUL: I prefer mountains actually.

ARNO: Well they say we're attracted to our opposites... you must want solidity.

PAUL: You think so?

ARNO: That's what those spiritual health books say.

PAUL: I must buy one.

ARNO: I went through a phase of reading that stuff.

PAUL: That's embarrassing.

ARNO: I read about ten in a row then I realised these people are psychotic.

PAUL: And greedy. That's a nice combination.

Silence.

ARNO: Do you pack your toothbrush when you go away?

PAUL: Away from home?

ARNO: Yeah.

PAUL: Yeah... usually... why?

ARNO: I always forget mine. I always have to buy one when I get there.

PAUL: That's so annoying.

ARNO: Yes it is... and in one of those books there's a whole paragraph about people like that.

Silence.

PAUL: Have you ever been to the Himalayas?

ARNO: No but I'd like to.

PAUL: I have. This five-day thing through Nepal.

ARNO: Must have been incredible.

PAUL: Yeah you're literally up there on top of the world.

ARNO: Was it fun?

PAUL: No. Not really. I wouldn't say fun.

ARNO: Why?

PAUL: Just the whole perspective. You're looking down at the earth sort of labouring... the way it squeezes and folds all these giant mountains like they're playdough or something. It's like flying over a city... but it's mountains... home to mythical demons.

ARNO: Wow.

PAUL: Yeah five days was as long as I could handle.

ARNO: Yeah?

PAUL: I couldn't have stayed longer. I would've left after the first day if it were possible. I had insomnia the whole time. I was shaking. At night my whole body was shaking. And when I slept I had these terrifying nightmares.

ARNO: What about the others?

PAUL: The other tourists?

ARNO: Yeah.

PAUL: They were all anxious too. No-one was talking to each other... it was weird. Except this Swiss guy. He beamed at everyone the whole time. Helped the guides do the cooking. The rest of us huddled in our tents. We hated him.

ARNO: Sounds like it was still worth it.

PAUL: Yes... it was extraordinary. When I came back I felt... I don't know how to describe it. I was enthused about... I was just happy... lighter... for a while.

   Silence.

I love the sound of playgrounds.

ARNO: Yeah.

PAUL: Wild isn't it?

ARNO: Soothing.

PAUL: Wild cacophony... like all these crazy birds or something.

ARNO: Cacophony of delight.

PAUL: There's an hysteria there... but it's okay.

ARNO: Yeah it's pure... thrill.

PAUL: Imagine being able to be as silly as you like. To express yourself so joyfully.

ARNO: The intensity of every experience.

PAUL: I mean someone out there's getting their first kiss.

ARNO: It's delightful isn't it?

PAUL: I like the way you can't distinguish any particular sound.

ARNO: Yeah.

PAUL: Like a yell. Is that one and a half sounds?

ARNO: Sort of confetti.

PAUL: Delight pouring through. And there's desperation too. Anxious to impress someone or...

ARNO: Pure delight.

PAUL: Yeah.

Silence.

Music is indescribable really isn't it?

ARNO: Yeah.

PAUL: Massages you.

ARNO: Yeah… it does.

PAUL: I read about these people getting tortured during the war and they got through it by imagining Mozart… Chopin…

ARNO: I can imagine.

Silence.

You know in Argentina… when they were torturing political prisoners… they'd play them Abba night and day.

PAUL: Jesus. That's harsh.

ARNO: They actually did that. Mind you if I were dying… I'd like some sort of music.

PAUL: Maybe you wouldn't need any.

ARNO: I'd like to go out with the Beach Boys.

PAUL: You're not planning on dying any time soon?

ARNO: No… not that I'm aware of.

PAUL: There've been times in my life where music has actually saved me.

ARNO: Yeah.

PAUL: When I feel flat or … it's music that lifts me out of it.

ARNO: Who do you put on?

PAUL: Usually it's just the classical station. Yaknow I get home it's late at night it's really quiet but I've got my headphones so I can turn it up yaknow full bore no-one can hear and I just sort of give myself over to the music let it hold me up for a while. Suddenly my little life is this great drama.

ARNO: That's why I started doing life-drawing classes.

PAUL: Oh okay. That's interesting.

ARNO: I just thought it would help me look at things… really look at things… the way children look at things… for the first time… the fascination…

PAUL: Did it work?

ARNO: Ah…no.

PAUL: Are you're still doing it?

ARNO: Yeah.

Silence.

I met this woman there. Nina. She's the most extraordinary person.
The most honest person I've ever met. But she's got no idea how to
function. No-one really knew her.

PAUL: Were you friends?

ARNO: Ah… I don't know. I bumped into her a few weeks back and she
invited me back to her place for a cup of tea. She's got this small flat
but it's really nice. Really comfy. She's really made it into something.
She's got really good taste. She has this amazing carving which she
said she picked up in West Africa. Six foot tall. God knows how she
got it back here.

PAUL: West Africa?

ARNO: Yeah. She has absolutely no self-confidence… incredibly insecure
but will tell you exactly what she's thinking.

PAUL: Which people don't like.

ARNO: That's why she's so lonely… and insecure. At first I used to think
it was for show… you know the way she tells you exactly what she's
thinking. But it's not.

Silence.

You know when it comes to health people always say… 'the Chinese
always say…' don't they?

SONG: 'O Thou Beloved'.

You ever been to confession?

PAUL: Like with a priest?

ARNO: Yeah.

PAUL: No.

ARNO: I've been a few times.

PAUL: Really?

ARNO: Yeah it's quite nerve-wracking actually.

PAUL: How funny is that?

ARNO: I like to get in there and see what the priest is up to. But all you
can really see are the lips moving. The first time I went I thought the
poor guy was trembling.

PAUL: Why would he be trembling?

ARNO: Because all I could see were the lips moving.
PAUL: Maybe he's praying.
ARNO: Yeah I'm not sure.
PAUL: So what do you tell him?
ARNO: My sins.
PAUL: Okay…
ARNO: Yeah.
PAUL: Sexual indiscretions?
ARNO: What's a sexual indiscretion?
PAUL: One you feel guilty about I guess.
ARNO: No no. I'm not into that. I'm not a believer. Just odd things like…
   when I was about twelve… my best friend at school was being spat
   on by this group of boys. They spat all over him. They spat in his
   sandwich and I just stood there and laughed.
PAUL: You laughed?
ARNO: Yeah. It's just one of those things I've never told anyone… but
   with the priest… I just did.
PAUL: We've all done things like that.
ARNO: Sure. You say what's convenient right?
PAUL: Well if you take a stance… about things you believe in… everyday
   life would crush you.
ARNO: But it wouldn't that's the thing.
PAUL: Look at your friend Nina… look what happened to her…
ARNO: What happened to her?
PAUL: … for being honest.
ARNO: Yeah but…
PAUL: People turn against you.
ARNO: You can't be honest all the time.
PAUL: Isn't that cowardice?
ARNO: It's too intimidating.
PAUL: And the result is a kind of passive cowardice towards
   everything.
ARNO: Yeah but that's kind of necessary.
PAUL: Even when I laugh or get angry I feel ridiculous.
ARNO: Why shouldn't you? Who are all these people… strangers every-
   where… friends who aren't really friends?

   Silence.

PAUL: You remember that guy who ploughed into those kids.

ARNO: About a year ago?

PAUL: They were coming home from a party. And this guy comes towards them... his car veers towards them and crashes into these kids. He massacred these kids... teenagers. And the guy's got a three-year-old in the front seat. He just gets out of the car and leaves him there... in the front seat and runs. He runs and hides in some bushes for a few hours. Of course he does. The papers all say how terrible... how appalling this man is. How could anyone... a human being do such a thing? An abominable thing. As though they... some journalist would know what it's like. He's a coward... yes... but who isn't? It's a perfectly natural reaction when you think about it. It's understandable. Who wants freedom? Who really wants total freedom? I mean really wants it?

ARNO: That's what I like about confession... to be able to tell someone... someone you can't see... whatever. It can be scary.

PAUL: I bet.

ARNO: Yeah it's like there's some great power there... behind this screen.

PAUL: I'd find it hilarious.

ARNO: That's what's scary. I often get the giggles.

PAUL: You laugh?

ARNO: Hmm. But when he asks me if there's anything I'd like to confess... and I just snap out of it and it all just tumbles. Everything I can think of... like I have no right to it. I have no right to anything in there in that fucking little room.

PAUL: Does he ever interrupt you?

ARNO: No no... just the lips moving. Afterwards they say a prayer. Tell you your sins are absolved. It's very simple. The things you carry around... for decades... gone.

PAUL: You think so?

ARNO: I feel terrific afterwards.

PAUL: I should give it a go.

ARNO: I recommend it for everyone.

   SONG: 'Peace'.

PAUL: I was talking to this guy the other day who doesn't speak English very well. And anyway he was saying this word and I couldn't understand him so he typed it into his phone… but I can't remember the fucking word. It's driving me mad.

ARNO: Yeah.

Silence.

Are you a drinker?

PAUL: No.

ARNO: No? Not at all?

PAUL: I'm not good to be around when I drink. My behaviour isn't reliable.

ARNO: What sort of things do you do?

PAUL: Oh nothing really I spent a lot of time rolling around in the garden apparently… groaning. Yaknow just urinating around the place. Now it's like I dunno I've got no shtick or something… everything is like just sort of one thing after another… sort of even… this smooth plain… yeah… it's really new… unfamiliar.

Silence.

I've being seeing a few films lately.

ARNO: Oh yeah.

PAUL: Am I imagining this or are films becoming more identical?

ARNO: Yeah.

PAUL: I feel like I'm seeing the same one over and over. Doesn't anybody have a memory?

ARNO: No. Maybe not.

PAUL: What's it about? Reassurance?

ARNO: Don't know. Maybe pity. When it's not the same people feel threatened.

Silence.

PAUL: I had this dream the other night I was driving along a highway. And then I realised I was in a Messerschmitt 109. So I took off and was flying around… over the city… diving and looping about… then I could see this balcony with people on it and I started flying straight toward it and then I just flew through it.

ARNO: Yeah.

PAUL: Yeah it was made of paper and then I came up and I was in another country.

Silence.

ARNO: Whereabouts?

PAUL: Well there was jungle.

ARNO: Jungle?

PAUL: Yeah.

ARNO: Could be anywhere.

PAUL: Yeah well it's a dream so...

Silence.

Apparently Mexican cinema is going through a renaissance.

ARNO: Yes I read that somewhere.

PAUL: Things always seem to be bubbling away in other places.

ARNO: What's happening here?

PAUL: I've got no idea. I really don't have any perspective on it.

Silence.

ARNO: I wrote a film script once.

PAUL: Yeah?

ARNO: Actually I didn't write it but I thought it up one day.

PAUL: For fun?

ARNO: I was thinking about the kind of film you'd never see. It was about a man who stayed indoors all the time. He was suicidal.

PAUL: Right.

ARNO: He was extremely fat. And he had a relationship with this hundred-year-old woman. She looked like a dried apricot.

PAUL: Doesn't sound too commercial.

ARNO: It was a kind of fairytale.

PAUL: Yes.

ARNO: They were in love. Absolutely head over heels. They danced and drank and frolicked. It all made sense... because apart from the obvious age difference they were perfectly matched. There was this pivotal moment... he began to talk about suicide with her... for the first time... he said deep down he wanted to die... had been thinking like that for a long time... he was sick of it. Sick of being himself... or what was expected of himself. He asked her... how did she keep going...? All those years...? How did she keep up her appetite?

PAUL: What did she say?

ARNO: Sex.

PAUL: Did they have sex?

ARNO: In the film?

PAUL: Yes.

ARNO: Yes but they couldn't find a good position so they gave up. Ate magic mushrooms instead. Real strong ones. Then there's this trippy moment in the film.

PAUL: What happened then?

ARNO: Nothing. Things didn't work out. He kept on being suicidal.

PAUL: So you didn't actually write it?

ARNO: No I said that.

Silence.

Bumped into an old teacher of mine recently. He was really a great teacher. And he loved science which is unusual for Catholics.

PAUL: I guess so. What do you mean?

ARNO: He used to teach us about the Big Bang theory and sunspots.

PAUL: Yeah?

ARNO: Saw him about a month ago at some exhibition.

PAUL: Okay.

ARNO: Saw him on the way in. Gave me a little nudge. I think he wanted to give me a hug. But I didn't recognise him at first. I held back. You know I was so shocked. It was horrific. To see him… this old… decrepit… broken man.

PAUL: Yeah.

ARNO: I could barely look at him.

PAUL: Did you chat?

ARNO: No. I wanted to get away as quickly as I could.

PAUL: I suppose it's inevitable.

ARNO: What is?

PAUL: These people… who live in order to help. They're bound to be disappointed. It's bound to destroy them in the end.

ARNO: I don't know about that.

PAUL: I'm just talking about religious people… what they believe in… their values have evaporated. Must make them think what a waste.

ARNO: He looked shattered… destroyed.

SONG: 'Thou, All My Bliss'.

I had this first job when I was about thirteen.

PAUL: Yeah?

ARNO: In a menswear store for well-to-do clientele.

PAUL: Okay.

ARNO: This woman came in… wanted to buy a tie for her husband or boyfriend whatever. I remember thinking she looked old… because I was so young.

PAUL: Don't think I've ever bought a tie.

ARNO: Yeah me neither. Not for me anyway. I don't like things around my neck.

PAUL: What about scarves?

ARNO: I don't like them either.

PAUL: That's unusual. I like them.

ARNO: Yeah? I didn't know what I was doing. It's my first job. So I ask her if the tie needs to match with anything… like a pair of shoes or a jacket or something… had she given this much thought… had she done her homework?

PAUL: Well you don't want to be reckless.

ARNO: Exactly. I asked her to make some choices. Once she'd selected a few I laid them out on the cabinet so we could see them.

PAUL: What were they like?

ARNO: The ties?

PAUL: Yeah.

ARNO: Garish. Garish taste. She was a really fun girl… spontaneous. And I said something like… look I may be young but as a guy there's just no way I would wear one of these… except maybe as some sort of joke thing. Is that what you want some sort of crazy thing?

PAUL: So what did she say to that?

ARNO: I didn't have a clue what I was talking about right? So I started asking questions about him. You know what was he like? Was he blonde… dark?

PAUL: And what was he like?

ARNO: She started telling me… she felt he didn't respect her…

PAUL: The husband?

ARNO: Yeah or boyfriend whatever… that he took her for granted. She said he didn't speak to her for days on end yet expected sex whenever he wanted it. And if she didn't want to he'd get angry.

PAUL: She told you all this? You're thirteen.

ARNO: Yeah… I know. She was telling me all this and then she started giggling. She kept calling him 'the coconut'. Whenever she said the word 'coconut' she'd go and pinch me hard on the arm. One time she did it I caught her by the finger and gave her a squeeze… really squeezed her finger and she cracked up laughing. We had a little tug of war right there in the shop. She pulled to free herself and I kept holding on. Then she gave a really hard tug and fell over backwards in the middle of the shop. I went to help her up and she just started pissing herself laughing.

PAUL: Sounds like a great place to work.

ARNO: Man it was a farce. I realised that right then because I found myself trying to convince her to not buy him a tie… to not buy him anything.

PAUL: And this is your first sale?

ARNO: Pretty much.

PAUL: What happened then?

ARNO: She decided to play a little trick. She bought the ugliest most revolting tie we had on offer. Bright orange with lime green firemen on it or something. Made out of mohair.

PAUL: You're joking.

ARNO: I wrapped it up… we were just pissing ourselves… everyone in the shop looking at us… we just laughed and laughed.

PAUL: That's great.

ARNO: Then I got fired.

PAUL: For laughing?

ARNO: Yep. I wonder what it was like for her? Falling over in the middle of a shop… pissing herself… with a thirteen-year-old?

Silence.

PAUL: It's amazing all these old traditions keep cropping up. Waiters wearing waistcoats in restaurants… uniforms cropping up everywhere you noticed that?

ARNO: Yeah.

PAUL: In lifts… department stores… even seven elevens they got these weird little uniforms.

ARNO: I saw in the paper they're advertising for butlers.

PAUL: Why would you want a butler?

ARNO: You would have to feel ridiculous.

PAUL: Imagine saying to someone… how's your butler by the way?
ARNO: You open a door and you've got a butler standing there.
PAUL: What do they do exactly? Apart from answering the door?
ARNO: Scratch your arse? I dunno.

Silence. ARNO *looks at* PAUL*'s wrist.*

What did you do to your forearm?
PAUL: I don't know.
ARNO: Nasty scar right there.
PAUL: Yeah I don't know.
ARNO: Nasty scar. What were you doing?
PAUL: When?
ARNO: Did you fall over?
PAUL: No… I don't know.

Silence.

I've been reading Hafiz lately.
ARNO: Who's that?
PAUL: One of those Sufi poets.
ARNO: I've heard of Rumi but not him.
PAUL: Oh he's great. There's this one that goes… 'where does poetry live…? in the eye that says wow…'
ARNO: You know this off by heart?
PAUL: Yeah.
ARNO: Sorry start again.
PAUL: Okay yeah… 'where does poetry live…? in the eye that says wow… in the overpowering splendour every mind knows when it realises… our life is only a few magic seconds…' sorry… 'our life dance is only a few magic seconds… from our heart shouting… I'm so alive'.
ARNO: Beautiful.
PAUL: Yeah… and he wrote like… seven hundred years ago.
ARNO: Do you often memorise poems?
PAUL: No not really. I think I know a little bit of Shakespeare and maybe a line from Dante.

ARNO *recites 'Otto's Mops' by Ernst Jandl.*

ARNO: It's about a dog that eats an orange and vomits.

PAUL: Yeah?

Silence.

ARNO: I tried to read the *Mahabharata* once. The Hindus know how to run a universe. It's all hands on deck.

Silence.

PAUL: I know this guy from Tehran… and he told me that over there they have these little shows in people's houses… poetry readings… performances… exhibitions… live music… stuff like that… and on any one night there might be five hundred of these gatherings going on. It's the only way to avoid censorship. But the thing is people have something they want to say.

ARNO: The repression nurtures the culture.

PAUL: In a funny way it must give you a sort of clarity.

ARNO: I guess here the issues are more complex. It's harder to pinpoint the enemy.

PAUL: Who's the enemy?

ARNO: I said it was complex.

PAUL: These guys breathe poetry.

ARNO: The Persians?

PAUL: At one point they controlled the whole of Asia Minor.

ARNO: Yes Xerxes and all that.

PAUL: Then along came Alexander the Great.

ARNO: Yeah and he fucked them.

Silence.

PAUL: A woman came up to me in the street and told me she loved me.

ARNO: Yeah? Did you know her?

PAUL: No.

ARNO: Was she deranged or…?

PAUL: I ended up talking with her for an hour.

ARNO: What about?

PAUL: She's about forty-five. She lives with her parents… out the back… in a caravan.

ARNO: Was she… you know okay?

PAUL: Mentally?

ARNO: Yeah.

PAUL: She was married… but her husband died in a freak accident rafting… white water rafting.

ARNO: Really?

PAUL: So she moved back to her parents. Yeah she left her house empty. She was quite wealthy but she couldn't live there anymore. So she and the daughter live in this caravan. She said it's like being on holiday.

ARNO: And why did she approach you like that?

PAUL: Well there's the charm factor.

Silence.

I've been going for a lot of walks lately.

ARNO: Anywhere in particular?

PAUL: No. Just around. Sometimes I'll catch a tram and get off and walk somewhere out of town… somewhere I haven't been before. People are fascinating… that's something you can depend on no matter where you go.

ARNO: Sure.

PAUL: Though hard to engage.

ARNO: Yes.

PAUL: They usually don't like to look at you.

ARNO: No.

PAUL: When I look at them… they invariably turn away.

ARNO: I have the same experience.

PAUL: It's hard to study someone's face with any intensity.

ARNO: You know what I find works?

PAUL: Tell me.

ARNO: Park yourself next to someone… anyone… and their friends or whatever… and just bore into their conversation.

PAUL: Yes I've done that.

ARNO: Can be a wild ride.

PAUL: Makes me feel deviant.

ARNO: Listening?

PAUL: Yeah.

ARNO: I wish it was that easy.

Silence.

PAUL: Do you ever pretend to be someone else?

ARNO: What...? Just make stuff up you mean?
PAUL: Yeah... when people ask about you?
ARNO: No.
PAUL: I often lie about myself.
ARNO: Yeah?
PAUL: All the time.
ARNO: What kind of things do you say?
PAUL: Well you can say anything. You could tell someone you're a detective working on a murder case and you've just discovered the body of an eighty-year-old man... sliced into pieces... you know and they've been put into manila folders in a filing cabinet. And now they're being posted out to people.
ARNO: But that's pretty silly. No-one would believe you.
PAUL: No but it's amazing because people expect you to tell the truth so...
ARNO: So you like taking the piss out of people?
PAUL: Just something I've always done.
ARNO: Since you were a kid?
PAUL: I don't know when it started.
ARNO: A confidence thing?
PAUL: Is it?
ARNO: How do you take someone seriously... if you're lying like that?
PAUL: Maybe they don't believe me.
ARNO: See what you can get away with?
PAUL: Sometimes.

    Silence.

The other day I was in this queue and there was this woman in front of me and I touched her hair. I dunno why I just touched her hair. Anyway she caught me... she turned around and caught me and I couldn't pretend I was doing something else so... but she was really good about it. We chatted and we introduced ourselves and... but I gave her a false name.

    Silence.

ARNO: What's that personality that always lies?
PAUL: What's that personality?
ARNO: You know personality?

PAUL: Personality… but what's that anyway…?

ARNO: What?

PAUL: The way people say your personality is this…?

ARNO: Yeah.

PAUL: Your character is that or… these qualities that are ascribed to you… before you know it… and then they cling to you…

ARNO: Yeah maybe.

PAUL: Qualities that are actually completely alien. That have nothing to do with you at all… but now you're expected to play along.

ARNO: Yeah right.

PAUL: You get to wear them for good… you know what I mean?

ARNO: These characteristics?

PAUL: Yeah.

ARNO: You can end up getting lost in it.

PAUL: Who can tell really? A person can be… a reserved… conservative person can suddenly laugh during someone's funeral.

ARNO: Yeah… I've seen it happen.

PAUL: Yeah I think it's quite common.

ARNO: This friend of mine. Really shy… incredibly shy. She went to her mother's funeral and laughed all the way through it pretty much.

PAUL: Great.

ARNO: From beginning to end. Afterwards I asked her if she was okay. She said yeah… it's liberating. It's a liberating day. At first I thought she meant for herself… I thought she must have been a domineering mother… but she said… 'no my mother is free… free of me'.

PAUL: That's great… she sounds nuts.

ARNO: No-one would've thought she was capable of doing that… not at her mother's funeral.

Silence.

Would you like to have kids?

PAUL: Yeah I'd like to?

ARNO: Yeah me too.

Silence.

You think kids grow up too fast?

PAUL: Compared to what?

Silence.

ARNO: I got on the train the other day and counted six adults reading *Harry Potter*.

PAUL: It's interesting with ageing… what's expected of you.

ARNO: Like what?

PAUL: I don't know… I'm just thinking with ageing… it's really about work… what we do… but how do you measure what you do? What you actually do? Where is the history? What's the difference between you… who say might be doing something for twenty years… compared to someone who's just starting now?

ARNO: Experience.

PAUL: Yes but how do you measure that?

ARNO: Is that important?

PAUL: People have these opinions of you… because of your work… it defines you… but you can't even measure it. It's all so fleeting.

ARNO: Perhaps you can measure it but no-one else can?

PAUL: But measure what?

ARNO: You have to be pretty sure of yourself… of what you know don't you?

PAUL: But who is so sure of themselves really?

ARNO: Some people are.

PAUL: Outwardly.

ARNO: That's why it's great to do jobs where you can see the result… the result of your work.

PAUL: Like what?

ARNO: Yeah when you can see something through… your project… from go to woe.

PAUL: So the work is captured? Put it into perspective?

ARNO: You need time… time to understand what it means to be honest with yourself. The knowledge that that entails.

PAUL: And then it all goes.

ARNO: And it's important to meet the customer… not some invisible name across the net.

PAUL: You think meeting the customer is a good thing?

ARNO: The interaction yes. What about these people who have their work scrutinised… consciously scrutinised… by strangers…?

PAUL: Like who?

ARNO: Like politicians say or… sportspeople…

PAUL: Yeah.

ARNO: Would have to make you more insecure on some level.

PAUL: That's what they train for.

ARNO: What about telemarketers...? These days everyone gets listened to by their supervisors... salespeople... office workers...

PAUL: There's always someone listening.

ARNO: Yes.

PAUL: Someone watching.

ARNO: Yes.

PAUL: When you're alone... watching yourself.

ARNO: Yes... well maybe.

PAUL: We're always conscious of being observed. We perform. I mean it's all an elaborate mask.

ARNO: Yeah maybe... more so for some people.

PAUL: What is it? Fear... of being watched... of showing yourself? Of being exposed? Why is it so necessary to hide?

ARNO: Perhaps the only time you really see someone's personality is when they're one or two... and then after that... as children... they learn to protect themselves by performing. But every now and then... you catch a glimpse of that two-year-old personality. It's like documentaries. People betray themselves in the most incredible ways without realising it.

PAUL: That's right.

ARNO: They're not trying to be interesting.

PAUL: But are they really not aware of performing?

ARNO: No. Often they are yes. Take a group of people like policemen... nurses... businessmen... junkies... musicians whatever. How often do you see them in places just where you'd expect to see them? And so often they're aware of the spectacle they're creating... playing the role. They virtually conform to the parody... the role we expect of them.

PAUL: Yeah but we all do that.

ARNO: But are we always conscious of it?

PAUL: Yeah I think... on a level... I mean there's always words that we're taught... clothes we wear... streets that have been designed for us to walk in... buildings... spaces designed for us to be in... the environment always implies a way of behaving... doesn't it? what's the difference? Where do you draw the line?

ARNO: It's about what people expect.
PAUL: People always expect a form of behaviour don't they?
ARNO: Yes.
PAUL: I mean you can't just go and lie down on the footpath can you?
ARNO: Really?
PAUL: Well you'd be arrested.
ARNO: That's not true.
PAUL: You'd be arrested for obstruction. You can't just go and lie down in a bank or an office building or a supermarket I mean that would just be enormously problematic for people.

Silence.

I saw this guy in the news who went home and shot up half his family.
ARNO: What was the reason?
PAUL: Nobody knows. They just had his face in the paper. Real mean looking bastard. Bald. Tatts. The cliché villain. And the whole thing was caught on camera.
ARNO: The murder?
PAUL: Yeah on this CTV camera.
ARNO: That'll go on the net.
PAUL: Yeah that's what they're saying.
ARNO: Who?
PAUL: The police. The guy did it purely to get into the papers.
ARNO: That's nothing new.
PAUL: Yeah but this guy addressed the camera while he was shooting these people. His whole family.
ARNO: He was obviously insane.
PAUL: Yeah but to be so aware of yourself … how you're coming across or something… your image… while doing something so horrific…it's just so weird.

Silence.

ARNO: What's your animal in the Chinese cosmology?
PAUL: Monkey.
ARNO: Me too.

Silence.

What's the morality of monkeys say… compared to human beings?

PAUL: Monkeys seem honest don't they?

ARNO: Do they?

PAUL: Yeah.

ARNO: No they're violent.

PAUL: Monkeys?

ARNO: Yeah.

PAUL: Do they commit genocide?

ARNO: Well they don't have the means. But if they did… you should see the way they hack into those macaroons.

PAUL: Macaroon?

ARNO: Yeah.

PAUL: That's a biscuit.

ARNO: Is it?

PAUL: Do you mean marmoset?

ARNO: Marmoset is it?

PAUL: Those weird little fury ones?

ARNO: Yeah.

Silence.

It's illegal to be cruel to a cat or a dog…

PAUL: Yeah…

ARNO: … but you can do what you like to a squid.

PAUL: There's this point where it becomes wrong.

ARNO: What animal do you think that is?

PAUL: Dunno.

ARNO: Has to be one of them.

Silence.

Is there something wrong with your eyes?

PAUL: Not that I know of.

ARNO: It's like you're sleeping with your eyes open.

PAUL: No. I'm okay.

ARNO: You look like you're asleep.

Silence.

Did you know the Tasmanian Aborigines would only count to five?

PAUL: Yeah?

ARNO: They went to five and after that… many.

PAUL: How do they know that?

ARNO: I read it somewhere.

PAUL: No I said how do they know that... given Truganini died what... a hundred and fifty years ago?

ARNO: What... historians?

PAUL: Yeah.

ARNO: They just know.

PAUL: What someone went round asking them what they could count to?

ARNO: Yeah why not?

PAUL: I find that hard to believe... given they shot most of them. I mean there wasn't much interest shown in their culture.

ARNO: Someone was interested.

PAUL: You think?

ARNO: It's what I read. An historical account. It's a nice idea... just count to five. Don't really need to count any more than that do we?

PAUL: Course you fucking do. How can you live in a city if you can't count more than five?

ARNO: There'd be a lot less pressure.

PAUL: What... anything more than five you feel tense?

ARNO: No.

> *Silence.*

It's a nice idea. Count to five and that's it.

> *SONG: 'For the Love My Heart Doth Prize'.*

PAUL: I went to Thailand a couple of years ago. Stayed in this bungalow. On a beach.

ARNO: Nice.

PAUL: In Ko Pha-Ngan.

ARNO: Oh yeah.

PAUL: I went for a wander one morning. The whole beach was empty because it was right in the middle of the monsoon... which I didn't know until I got there.

ARNO: You didn't do your research.

PAUL: There was this woman ahead of me looking down at the sand. When I got close she bent down and picked something up... and I looked at her and she smiled at me. I said to her oh is that a bit of coral? And she said no I don't think so... looks like a bit of plastic.

She came over and showed me and she was right. Looked like a piece of old bucket or something.

ARNO: It's amazing what the sea washes up.

PAUL: I took it off her and put it in my pocket and I leant over and kissed her. A really long kiss. The kind you dream about.

ARNO: Easy to misconstrue these things.

PAUL: One day... two years later... we walked past each other in the street.

ARNO: This was back here?

PAUL: She recognised me straight away. I had a bit of difficulty because she'd cut her hair short... which suits her better. But otherwise she was the same. Same mouth... same eyes.

ARNO: Was she happy to see you?

PAUL: She asked me if I remembered going to this hut. She described it. It was where fishermen used to hang their nets. I said no... but she continued to describe it in minute detail. In one alcove there was a statue of a sea monster... made of painted wood... and its hair was made out of knives... and it had a girl between its teeth and she had a red ball in her hand which was supposed to signify something.

ARNO: And you didn't remember any of this?

PAUL: No.

ARNO: Maybe you spent the whole day with her.

PAUL: She was telling me all this and then she looked at me and said sorry and I said no... no it's not your fault. I couldn't think of anything to say so I said... why don't we go for a drive? She said sure. We drove around for hours. Into the night. Eventually I said do you want to go home? She said no... it's alright... she'd been getting insomnia lately.

ARNO: Where did you go?

PAUL: We kept driving... talking a bit... but mostly in silence... around various suburbs. All these houses that seem vaguely familiar. One street had orange trees on the nature strip. At one point... it must have been about eleven thirty by now... she suggested we go inside someone's house.

ARNO: You mean break in?

PAUL: No she wanted to just pick one and go knock on the door.

ARNO: Anyone's?

PAUL: Yeah. She saw one. A typical fifties style… brick veneer… there was a gate… and when we opened it a light switched on over the path. The door opened. A woman opened it. It was like she was waiting for us. Some woman in her fifties. And my friend said to her… is it okay if we come in… we're new in town… and we just want to meet someone.

ARNO: What did she say?

PAUL: She lead us into the lounge room. The furniture. It was all the same colour. And very spaced apart.

ARNO: You're dreaming aren't you?

Silence.

PAUL: We were invited to sit down. The woman offered us a drink… it was greenish…. I took off my shoes. And I go and lie down. My friend comes and lies down next to me. The woman starts talking. Or singing… something… I can't remember. She just keeps singing… or talking…

Silence.

What are you looking at?

ARNO: Just your face.

Silence.

PAUL: I've been making a list.

ARNO: Oh yeah?

PAUL: Yeah of activities… things I'd like to do.

ARNO: Like what?

PAUL: I'm gonna go to the nursery and get some pot plants for my flowerbox thingo. I wanna get hold of these videos that teach you how to play guitar. Apparently they're excellent. Do you know about this Hawaiian massage? It's supposed to be amazing. It's called Lomi Lomi. It works on some kind of wave principle apparently. I'm getting one of those.

Silence.

Do you ever wish you could travel back in time?

ARNO: Yeah I do actually.

PAUL: I always think what it would be like at these famous rock gigs. You know being there… it's the Sex Pistols nineteen seventy-six…

you're right there. Or even Bruce Springsteen. I'm not a big fan but some of those concerts he played in New Jersey were so full-on apparently people couldn't go back to their lives. James Brown New York nineteen eighty-two... the gig that changed everything.

ARNO: Bahm bahm bahm bahm bahm. Boom da dum. I'd like to live in one of those Khmer temples.

PAUL: It'd be peaceful.

ARNO: It'd be noisy. The jungle is a noisy place.

PAUL: Only when it's raining.

ARNO: No all the time. There's insects eating things... birds... animals... all the shrieks.

PAUL: I'd like to live with a colony of seals.

ARNO: What... as a seal?

PAUL: Yeah.

ARNO: They've got a lazy life haven't they?

PAUL: You seen how fast they swim?

ARNO: They have to catch fish.

PAUL: Yeah... fresh fish all day long.

Silence.

ARNO: Can I have a look at your hands?

PAUL: Why?

ARNO: I just want to have a look.

PAUL: You read palms?

ARNO: No. Your fingers are long.

PAUL: Yeah I guess.

ARNO: Mine are a lot more fleshy.

PAUL: If you had really hairy hands would you wax them?

ARNO: What do you mean?

PAUL: Big clumps of black hair.

ARNO: On my hands?

PAUL: Yeah.

ARNO: No probably not.

PAUL: I find it disgusting.

ARNO: Are you scared of spiders?

PAUL: You think that's what it's about?

ARNO: Maybe... maybe.

PAUL: The Assyrians used to collect them.

ARNO: Hands?

PAUL: Yeah after a battle. That's how they counted the dead. They'd lay them out in the square and all the citizens would gather around and celebrate. Sing songs. And they used to dry them out. A special process. A slow bake. People could buy them. Take them home and put them on the fridge... hang them around the bedpost.

ARNO: Make them feel safe.

PAUL: Yeah.

> *Silence.*

How much energy goes into worrying about offending people? Sometimes I've bought something... something I don't want because I was worried about offending the shopkeeper.

ARNO: Yes.

PAUL: Sometimes I put things on lay-by and don't go back.

ARNO: Jesus.

PAUL: You done that?

ARNO: Yes.

PAUL: Right now I'm on a mission to buy a really good mug.

ARNO: A cup?

PAUL: Yeah it's quite difficult to get one that's just right. I want to get one that's just right. That suits me yaknow. If you think about it it's probably the thing that I pick up most... out of any other object in my flat.... it's the one thing I'm most attracted to.

ARNO: Yes.

PAUL: It's the most intimate object.

ARNO: You drink from it so...

PAUL: How many times do I put my lips on it each day?

ARNO: Fifty to a hundred?

PAUL: Easily so... I'm willing to pay quite a bit.

ARNO: How would you sell a mug?

PAUL: In a shop?

ARNO: Yeah.

PAUL: You can't.

ARNO: No?

PAUL: A mug can only sell itself. To you. It's your mouth. The right mouth. The right mouth comes along for it.

ARNO: How long have you been looking?

PAUL: A few weeks.

ARNO: You haven't found the right one?

PAUL: Obviously not.

ARNO: You're willing to pay a princely sum?

PAUL: A princely sum.

ARNO: I'm more in the process of shedding things.

PAUL: Right now?

ARNO: Yeah.

PAUL: Shedding possessions?

ARNO: Yes.

PAUL: Do you have too many?

ARNO: No I don't think so. Probably less than most people. But there's always more to get rid of. A few more rooms to disembowel before I'm happy. Then the job's done. Do you need anything?

PAUL: Not really.

ARNO: I've got this old antique rocking horse. Had it for ages.

PAUL: An old one?

ARNO: Yeah. You want it?

PAUL: No I'm okay thanks.

ARNO: Do you need a chest of drawers?

PAUL: You don't need it?

ARNO: Not really.

PAUL: I think I'm okay.

ARNO: It's a nice one.

PAUL: I've got one. It's fine.

ARNO: I want the place to be more or less empty.

PAUL: Okay.

ARNO: I want to use less. Just what I need.

PAUL: Like a monk?

ARNO: No nothing like that. No it started... actually it started... I was eating in a restaurant with a friend... and we overheard this conversation. These people at the next table... people in their twenties talking about how to make money.

PAUL: Yeah.

ARNO: Then one of the guys starts saying to this other one... why do you buy all these old bottles of wine? It's stupid... there are much better ways to make money. Then other guy says... look I know it's not a good investment.

PAUL: I thought wine was a good investment.

ARNO: I don't know. And he says... the reason I buy these old bottles is because for two years I was a manic depressive... I was suicidal for two years. The wine is what saved me. I wanted to be around to open it. I couldn't bear dying without knowing what it tasted like. He actually said that. I couldn't bear dying without knowing what it tasted like. The conversation sort of ground to a halt after that... one of them went to the bathroom and then after that we really couldn't hear what they were saying. And a few days later I was lying about... I looked around and saw this old lamp sitting in the corner and I picked it up and took it outside and put it on the verge.

PAUL: The verge?

ARNO: Yeah you know. The verge. The grass strip between the road and the footpath. Then I went inside and made a cup of tea or something and I came out a few minutes later and it was gone. I thought... what else can I make disappear? I went round the house looking for stuff. I found some old boots... some books and clothes... an old bookcase and I put them outside... on the verge. Couple of hours later... all gone. It's harder to find things to throw out now. Now the initial rush is over. I have to really think about it... really consider if I want to keep it or throw it away.

PAUL: Have you been suicidal?

ARNO: No not at all.

PAUL: Depressed?

ARNO: No not at all.

   Silence.

PAUL: I'd like to sleep on people's couches again.

ARNO: So would I.

PAUL: Just crash out anywhere like that... sleep in any position.

ARNO: Nothing's stopping you though is there?

PAUL: I guess not.

   AV: A ship passing slowly.

   SONG: 'To Be Near One's Beloved'.

ARNO: I hate going to sleep. I get by on about four hours a night. I have a strong black coffee before I got to bed... around three in the morning... and then I just conk out.

PAUL: Despite the caffeine?

ARNO: Caffeine knocks me out at three in the morning. When I wake up I swing out of bed. No dream. Four hours wasted. I like the nights. I work better at night.

PAUL: My cat goes on an adventure every night.

ARNO: Do you ever follow him?

PAUL: Yes but he's too quick.

ARNO: And he has night vision.

PAUL: He sneaks under cars.

ARNO: What's its name?

PAUL: Muni.

ARNO: Nice name.

PAUL: Thanks.

ARNO: You know when people go and give themselves a new name… they always pick names like Cabbage or… Esmerelda Seventeen.

PAUL: I knew a guy once called Tall Building.

ARNO: What? What was his first name?

PAUL: Tall.

ARNO: So you called him Tall?

PAUL: Yeah. Are there any names you like?

ARNO: I like Arthur.

PAUL: Why?

ARNO: I don't know.

PAUL: It's not very adventurous.

ARNO: I like it.

PAUL: Tall is an adventurous name.

ARNO: Yes.

Silence.

PAUL: You have any memories of being in a cot?

ARNO: No.

PAUL: I remember my parents checking on me… making sure I wasn't being smothered by the pet cat.

ARNO: My earliest memory is dragging a stick across the lawn.

PAUL: What kind of stick?

ARNO: Just a stick.

Silence.

I often have this compulsion... when I'm in a crowd... like a lift or something... to blow air at people. You know like blowing out a candle. I really have to stop myself from doing it... this compulsion.

Silence.

You look tired.

PAUL: I haven't been sleeping.

ARNO: When I had trouble sleeping once I put up a hammock in the lounge room.

PAUL: Did that help?

ARNO: It was like being in a cabin in a ship. A wooden ship. 'He said everything... everything he wanted to say. Everything was retrievable and he went for it.'

PAUL: What's that?

ARNO: Oh it's just something I read.

ARNO: What are you going to do?

PAUL: I don't know.

Silence.

When you're very tired... when you go beyond a certain point... images start floating in front of your eyes. I really like it.

ARNO: You okay?

PAUL: Yeah I'm fine.

Silence.

Have you still got that stick?

ARNO: No. No of course not.

Silence.

Do you know this? [*He hums a tune.*] Does it mean anything?

PAUL: No. I don't know it.

ARNO: The melody's kind of melancholic. The lyrics are really uplifting.

PAUL: You can't remember it?

ARNO: No I can't.

PAUL: No? I can't remember jokes either.

ARNO: I hate it when people tell jokes. It's impossible to talk to people who think they're funny. I went out with a girl like that once. Why do you want to be funny?

Silence.

You have a remarkable posture.
PAUL: You think?
ARNO: Yes. Perfectly straight back.
PAUL: Thank you.

He sits up straight.

THE END

HOLIDAY

BY RAIMONDO CORTESE

Cast
Paul Lum
Patrick Moffatt

Production
Concept/Direction Adriano Cortese
Text Raimondo Cortese
Set Anna Tregloan
Lighting Niklas Pajanti
Sound David Franzke
Dramaturgy Adriano Cortese, Paul Lum and Patrick Moffatt
Stage Manager Gordon Rymer
Ranters Theatre General Manager Alison Halit

Griffin Theatre Company's season of HOLIDAY
opened at the SBW Stables Theatre, Sydney on 6 February 2009.

HOLIDAY was first performed at Arts House, North Melbourne on 9 August 2007.

Photo Olivia Martin-McGuire *Design* Jeremy Saunders

GRIFFIN THEATRE COMPANY

THE SBW STABLES THEATRE

Incredibly, 2009 marks the thirtieth anniversary of Griffin Theatre Company's residency at the SBW Stables Theatre. For three decades, from its diamond stage in Kings Cross, Australia's leading new writing theatre has been a small but spirited engine room, consistently breaking new ground to create theatre experiences that are innovative, thrilling, provocative and transformational.

Back in 1986, playwright Michael Gow launched his career at Griffin with AWAY – now Australia's most performed play. The hit films LANTANA and THE BOYS began life as plays first produced here, as did the television series HEARTBREAK HIGH. Premiere productions, such as WOLF LULLABY, KAFKA DANCES, THE STORY OF THE MIRACLES AT COOKIE'S TABLE and HOLDING THE MAN continue to reaffirm Griffin's claim as a place of good beginnings.

Looking forward, Griffin is preparing for the next three decades, with a playwrights' residency and artistic development programs offering opportunity to new theatre-makers, and its ambassador and education programs providing access to new audiences.

Now, as Griffin realises its role as a national theatre for new writing, it will regularly tour its productions around the country and – through Griffin Independent– promote a creative dialogue between playwrights from Australia and the rest of the world.

Griffin Theatre Company is proud to manage and curate the SBW Stables Theatre on behalf of its owner the Seaborn Broughton and Walford Foundation. One of the great birthplaces of contemporary Australian theatre, it was the original home of the legendary Nimrod Theatre Company. With a capacity of only 120, it is also Sydney's most intimate and persuasive professional stage.

The SBW Foundation (established at the instigation of the late Dr Rodney Seaborn AO OBE) purchased the Stables in 1986, rescuing it from demolition and securing Griffin a home when its future in the venue was in jeopardy. Griffin acknowledges the generosity of the SBW Foundation in allowing it, since 1986, the use of the SBW Stables theatre rent free, less outgoings.

Griffin Theatre Company
13 Craigend Street, Kings Cross NSW 2011
Phone: 02 9332 1052
Fax: 02 9331 1524
Email: info@griffintheatre.com.au
Web: www.griffintheatre.com.au
SBW Stables Theatre
10 Nimrod Street, Kings Cross NSW 2011
Box Office: 02 8002 4772
Online booking at www.griffintheatre.com.au

RAIMONDO CORTESE
Playwright

For **Griffin Theatre Company**: *The Fertility of Objects*. **Other theatre**: For Ranters and Napier St Theatre: *Lucrezia and Cesare*; toured to Directors Cut, regional Vic. For Ranters: *The Room*. For Ranters and La Mama Theatre: *The Fertility of Objects*. For Ranters and 1997 Melbourne International Arts Festival: *Features of Blown Youth*; toured to Performance Space and Theater Der Welt, Berlin. For Ranters and Adelaide Arts Festival: *Roulette – a series of 12 two-handers*; toured to Company B Belvoir St, PoNTI Festival and Chapel off Chapel, Melb. For Ranters, Federation Festival and Playbox: *St. Kilda Tales;* toured to UK, and Teatro S.Joao and SITE Festival, Portugal. For Ranters and the 2003 Melbourne International Festival: *The Wall;* toured to Chaper Studio, Wales. For Ranters and Arts House: *Holiday;* remounted Malthouse Theatre. For Ranters and Chapter Studio: *Affection,* For Company B: *Threepenny Opera.* **Short Stories:** *The Indestructible Corpse.* **Positions:** Teacher of Script Writing and Improvisation at Melbourne University, Victorian College of the Arts and Victoria University. **Awards:** Green Room Award: Best New Australian Writing for Holiday (2007). **Training**: Victorian College of the Arts.

ADRIANO CORTESE
Director

For **Griffin Theatre Company**: Debut. **Other Theatre**: For Ranters Theatre: *Lucrezia and Cesare, Features of Blown Youth, Roulette Parts I* and *II, St Kilda Tales, The Wall, Affection, Holiday.* **As Actor:** For Ranters Theatre: *Roulette Part III.* For Melbourne Theatre Company: *Betrayal, Gift of the Gorgon, The Lady from the Sea.* For Sydney Theatre Company and Q Theatre: *Macbeth.* For Q Theatre and Ensemble Theatre: *The Quartette from Rigoletto.* For State Theatre Company of South Australia: *Six Characters in Search of an Author.* For Playbox Theatre: *Strangers in the Night.* **Film**: *Amy, Maidenhead, The Jammed.* **Awards:** Green Room Award for Best Director for *Holiday* (2008), Nomination for Green Room Award for *Roulette Parts I and II* and *St Kilda Tales.*

PATRICK MOFFATT
Performer

For **Griffin Theatre Company:** Debut. **Other Theatre:** For Ranters Theatre: *Holiday, Features of Blown Youth, The Fertility of Objects, St Kilda Tales, The Wall, Affection.* For Melbourne Theatre Company: *Away, Blabbermouth.* For Miettia's: *My Dinner with Andre.* For Janes/Bettinson Theatre UK: *Buddy, The Musical* – Australia and NZ. For Elston and Hocking: *Wind in the Willows.* For Swy Theatre Company: *Children of War.* **Music/Bands:** *Melody Lords, Elroy Flicker and the Fitzroy Gutterslugs, Une Planche D'Oeufs, Mein Egg, Four Way Street.* **Awards:** Green Room Award for Best Actor for *Holiday* (2008). **Training:** Victorian College of the Arts.

PAUL LUM
Performer

For **Griffin Theatre Company:** Debut. **Other Theatre:** For Ranters Theatre: *Holiday, Affection, The Wall, St Kilda Tales, Roulette.* For Malthouse Theatre: *Sex Diary of an Infidel .* For La Mama: *The Inner Sanctum.* For Melbourne Theatre Company: *Much Ado About Nothing, Othello, The Dutch Courtesan.* For NORPA: *The Flood.* For Punctum: *The Shed.* For The Universal: *In Angel Gear.* For Kickhouse: *Grace Among the Christians* **Training**: Victorian College of the Arts.

ANNA TREGLOAN
Set Design

For **Griffin Theatre Company:** Debut. **Other Theatre:** For Arena Theatre Company: *gamegirl, Eat Your Young, Panacea.* For Back to Back Theatre Company: *Mental, Mind's Eye.* For Caroline Lee: *The Three Interiors of Lola Strong, Alias Grace.* For Chunky Move: *Fleshmeat.* For Danceworks: *varrious.* For Lucy Guerin Inc.: *Heavy.* For MTC: *Art and Soul.* For Malthouse Theatre: *Kitten, Vamp, Venus and Adonis, Tartuffe, The Telltale Heart, Criminology, Sleeping Beauty, BLACK, Babes in the Wood, Eldorado, The Odyssey, The Ham Funeral, Journal of the Plague Year.* For Ranter's Theatre: *Holiday, St Kilda Tales.* For Chamber Made: *The Hive.* For Moira Finucane: *Gotharama, The Saucy Canteena.* **As Co-Creator:** For Malthouse Theatre: *Sleeping Beauty.* **As director/creator:** For anarko and Malthouse Theatre: *BLACK.* For anarko: *Contemptuous Perplexity, The Long Slow Death of A Porn Star, Skin Flick, Body Function, The*

Church of Perpetual Motion, Mach. **Positions**: Resident Artist at Malthouse Theatre, Associate Artist of the Storeroom Theatre Workshop. **Awards:** Green Room Association Awards for Most Outstanding Designs (2005, 2007), John Truscott Award for Excellence in Design (2005), Helpmann Award for Best Design (2006).

NIKLAS PAJANTI
Lighting Designer

For **Griffin Theatre Company**: Debut. **Other theatre**: For Ballet Lab: *Axeman Lullaby.* For Black Arm Band/ Melbourne International Arts Festival*: Murundak.* For Brink Productions*: When the Rain Stops Falling.* For Chunky Move: *I Want to Dance Better at Parties, Singularity, Tense Dave, Three's a Crowd.* For Company B: *Yibiyung, The Pillowman, Who's Afraid of Virginia Woolf.* For The Eleventh Hour: *Endgame, Not What I am – Othello Retold, Winter's Tale, King John, The Crucible, Yet Each Man Kills the Thing He Loves, Because of the Increasing Disorder.* For Kage: A*ppetite.* For Malthouse Theatre: *Kitten, Not Like Beckett.* For Not Yet It's Difficult: *The Meaning of Moorabbin is Open For Inspection.* For The Rabble: *Osama the Hero.* For Ranters Theatre: *Holiday.* For Shaun Parker/Marguerite Pepper/Melbourne International Arts Festival: *This Show Is About People.* For Token Events: *Frank Woodley – Possessed, Spicks and Speck-tacular, Lano and Woodley – Goodbye.* **As Assistant Lighting Designer:** For Chamber Made: *Teorema, The Hive* and *Crossing Live.* For Not Yet It's Difficult: *Scenes of the Beginning from the End* and *K.* **Positions:** Principal Lighting Designer for trafficlight. **Awards**: Victorian Green Room Award for Lighting Dance. Nominations for Victorian Green Room Awards in the categories of Theatre, Opera and Dance. Nomination for Helpmann Industry Award for Best Lighting Design. **Training**: Victorian College of the Arts, Royal Melbourne Institute of Technology.

DAVID FRANZKE
Sound Designer

Griffin Theatre Company: Debut. **Digital Video Installations:** For Australian Centre for Contemporary Art/Art Gallery of New South Wales: *Untouchable*. For Australian Centre of the Moving Image: *Maniac de Luxe*. For Conical Gallery: *Exhausted Nature*. With Daniel Crooks: *Static no. 11 (man running)*. With David Rosetzky: *No Fear, Nothing Like This*. For National Gallery of Victoria: *Without You*. **Awards:** Green Room Award for Outstanding Work in Fringe Theatre for SkinFlick, Basil Sellers Sports/Arts Prize (2008). Anne Landa Award for *Untouchable* (2005).

GORDON RYMER
Stage Manager

For **Griffin Theatre Company:** *China*; toured to Adelaide, Melbourne, Stavanger, Bergen, Brussels, Lisbon, Halle, Dunedin & Nelson. **Other theatre:** For Performing Lines: *China*. For Sydney Opera House: *Objects for Meditation*; toured to Brussels, Brisbane, Oslo, Rotterdam, Lyon, Reunion Island, Singapore & Melbourne. For Sydney Opera House and Brisbane Powerhouse: *Flash Blak*. For Bell Shakespeare Company: *Twelfth Night*. For Performing Lines: *From the Inside Out, My Generation*. For B Sharp: *Loveplay*. For Glass Theatre: *Sugarbomb*. For Shaughna E Carter Productions: *Twelfth Night*. **Other positions:** Stage Manager & Assistant Precinct Co-ordinator for *World Youth Day 2008*. Site Manager for *Dawn Service* 2008, VP Celebrations 2005 & Athens Torch Relay 2004; Production Manger for *Australia Day 2008 & 2007, Remembrance Day Service 2007*; Production Assistant for *Commonwealth Day Service 2006* OPSE. Project Co-ordinator for *APEC 2007*. Game Day Floor Manager for *Sydney Swans 2004-2007*. **Training:** NIDA (Technical Production, 2003).

GRIFFIN THEATRE COMPANY

GRIFFIN DONORS

Principal Sponsor

Chartered Accountants
& Business Advisers

Production Partner

Company Partners

Artistic Partners

Exclusive Media Partner

Honorary Auditors

Rosenfeld,
Kant&Co.

SBW Stables Theatre Owned By

Government Partners

Griffin Theatre Company is assisted by the Australian Government through the Australia Council, its arts funding and advisory body; and the NSW Government through Arts NSW.

Go to the theatre more often...

Interesting Fact #1

Did you know people carry around different running tabs in their heads?

You have, for example, an "entertainment account." Losing a theatre ticket and replacing it costs your entertainment account $100 instead of the planned $50. Lost cash, however, is charged to another account - which is why most people would replace a theatre ticket even after they lost some cash but not if they lost a ticket.

The $50 theatre ticket should be equal to the $50 cash, but human beings don't think this way, which is why economic models of human behaviour often turn out to be wrong.

Thinking like an accountant can free you up to enjoy all that life has to offer

For expert financial advice Tel: 1300 753 222

Patrick Moffatt and Paul Lum in the Ranters Theatre production of Holiday *at Arts House in Melbourne.*